Contents

WHAT'S WRONG?

When you have a cold coming, you may feel tired and have no energy for a few days. Your throat may start to feel sore or tickly. Sometimes you feel hot and flushed and sometimes cold and shivery.

6

Did you know?

When you shiver, your body shakes to try to warm up. Tiny *muscles* pull the hairs on your skin upright.

feeling ill?

Coughs and Colds

By Jillian Powell

Dear Doc

I think I've got a cold coming. What can I do?

Drink plenty, take some vitamin C, and go to bed early so your body can rest.

7

CATCHING A COLD

Everyone gets colds sometimes.
You catch them from tiny **germs**
in the air or on things you touch.
They are spread by coughing
and sneezing or by touch.
Your body fights off lots of
germs every day, but if you feel
tired or run-down, you may still
catch a cold.

Did you know?

Germs can get
into our bodies
when we touch
our nose or eyes.

I caught a cold from my friend Kieran. He sits next to me in class. Then I gave my cold to my brother Danny at home!

Mum took my temperature because I felt hot. We read the **thermometer**.

It showed I had a fever because of my cold.

WHAT'S GOING ON?

You may feel hot because you have a **fever**. Your body temperature is normally 37°C. It goes up when your body is fighting a **virus**. The cold virus begins to multiply inside your nose and throat. Your throat may feel sore. You feel tired because your body is telling you it needs rest.

Did you know?

Your body sweats to cool itself down. Sweat cools you as it dries on your skin.

FIGHTING A COLD

Your body begins to flush out the germs. It makes a sticky mucus in your nose and throat. This makes your nose runny or blocked. Sometimes your eyes run too. You start sneezing or coughing as your body tries to clear your **airways**.

Dear Doc

My nose is really blocked and it's hard to breathe. What can I do?

Ask an adult to put a drop of menthol in boiled water for you and then breathe in the steam.

Cold germs pass into your blood too. Your body makes more **white blood cells** to fight them.

GETTING BETTER

Drinking plenty of water and fruit juice will help if you have a fever. You may not feel hungry but you should try to eat if you can. Rest, so that your body can use the energy to fight the virus. There are no medicines to cure colds but some can help you breathe or sleep more easily.

Did you know?

People who smoke catch more colds than non-smokers.

14

Ella's story

When I got a bad cold, Dad made me lots of warm drinks with honey and lemon juice. Lemons contain lots of vitamin C.

15

GETTING A COUGH

Sometimes you get a cough with a cold. Coughing is your body's way of trying to clear your airways. When you have a cold, you cough to try to clear **mucus** from your throat and lungs. You can take cough sweets and medicine to help soothe a cough that troubles you.

16

Dear Doc

I've got a bad cough that comes on at night. What can I do?

Before you go to bed, have a warm drink made with honey or sage.

Ben's story

I went to the doctor's because I had a bad cough. She listened to my chest and gave me some medicine to help me get rid of the cough.

COLDS AND HYGIENE

You can help stop germs spreading by taking care with **hygiene**. Always cover your mouth when you cough or sneeze. A cold virus spreads through tiny droplets in the air.

Dear Doc

My nose is red and sore from blowing it all the time! What can I do?

Try putting a little Vaseline under your nose and use gentle tissues that have balm in them.

You can catch a virus if you touch something that has germs on it and then you touch your mouth. Always wash your hands before you eat anything.

STAYING FIT

You can boost your **immune system** by looking after yourself. Doing sports can help to boost the immune system. This is because your body makes more white blood cells when you exercise.

Dear Doc

My mum bought a *nasal spray* to stop us getting colds. How do they work?

They coat the germs inside your nose with a gel before they can multiply.

Eat healthy foods like fresh fruit and vegetables. They contain vitamin C to help you fight germs.

Did you know?

A kiwi fruit contains all the vitamin C you need in a day!

21

Glossary

Airways	the tubes that lead from our throat to our lungs
Balm	an oil or lotion made from plants that soothes or calms the skin
Fever	having a high body temperature due to an illness
Germs	tiny living things that can cause illnesses
Hygiene	keeping the body clean and free from germs
Immune system	parts of the body that fight infection
Menthol	a substance made from peppermint oil that helps clear our airways
Mucus	sticky stuff made in the body, also called phlegm
Muscles	tissue in your body that you use to move different body parts
Nasal spray	a medicine spray for the nose
Thermometer	a temperature scale for reading someone's body temperature
Virus	a germ that multiplies inside body cells
Vitamin C	a substance found in foods including fruits and vegetables that we need to stay healthy and fight illnesses
White blood cells	cells in our blood and other body parts that attack and kill germs